MILITARY AIRCRAFT IN COLOUR

Hiroshi Seo

First published in 1984 by
Yama-kei Publishers Co. Ltd. Tokyo, Japan

Photographs © Hiroshi Seo, 1984

Text © Jane's Publishing Company Limited 1985

First published in the United Kingdom
in 1985 by Jane's Publishing Company Limited
238 City Road, London EC1V 2PU

ISBN 0 7106 0345 2

Distributed in the Philippines
and the USA and its dependencies by
Jane's Publishing Inc
135 West 50th Street
New York, NY 10020

Printed in Japan

JANE'S

Contents

Foreword

This unique illustrated volume contains selected colour
photographs and brief descriptions of major military aircraft of the
world, except those of the Soviet block. Also omitted are unarmed
trainers and liaison aircraft, while only the principal transport aircraft
types are covered.

However, several pages are devoted to each of the more
important aircraft types to show their variants from different angles.

Hiroshi Seo is a Japanese photographer who has specialised in
aviation, and the outstanding quality of his camera work is reflected
in these pages. Many of his photographs were taken in the air,
including some from the 'second seat' of supersonic fighters.

For the technically interested, each photographic reproduction of
the author's colour slides is accompanied by details of the lens size,
f-number, exposure and type of film used, where KM = Kodachrome
25 and KR = Kodachrome 64. The photographer has used Nikon
equipment throughout.

Grumman F-14 Tomcat Two-seat fleet defence and air superiority fighter of the US Navy. Automatically controlled swing-wing system provides outstanding manoeuvrability and good loiter and take-off/landing performance.

F-14A launches from the catapult of USS Ranger *off the coast of Hawaii in April 1980.   400 mm f8 1/500 KR*

Grumman F-14 Tomcat F-14A is equipped with AWG-9 fire control system which can track 24 targets and fire Phoenix long-range air-to-air missiles against six enemy aircraft simultaneously. **Span** 19.54/10.15 m (64 ft 1½ in/33 ft 3½ in) **Length** (overall) 19.10 m (62 ft 8 in) **Max speed** Mach 2.34

F-14A is high-speed configuration at NAS Point Mugu on the 'Open Day' in October 1979.   400 mm f5.6 + ²/₃ 1/500 KR

Grumman F-14 Tomcat F-14A was first flown in December 1970, and the first two Tomcat squadrons were commissioned in October 1972. Production of the advanced F-14D equipped with more powerful engines and improved avionics is planned for mid-1980s.

Two Tomcat squadrons deployed aboard USS Carl Vinson, *photographed from Cessna 172 at Sasebo, Japan, in October 1983.*   *180 mm f5.6 1/500 KR*

McDonnell Douglas F-15 Eagle Air superiority fighter, developed for the USAF to replace the F-4 Phantom. Of outstanding flight performance, the F-15 is equipped with the latest technology fire control radar and air-to-air armament. F-15 Eagles are also operated by the air forces of Israel, Japan and Saudi Arabia.

Nocturnal flight line-up of JASDF's F-15s at Nyutabaru AB in October 1983.   105 mm f8 Auto KR

McDonnell Douglas F-15 Eagle McDonnell Douglas F-15 Eagle is the USAF's first air superiority fighter since the F-86 Sabre, which played a major role in the Korean War. After that conflict, as fighters became supersonic and their armament began to include advanced radar equipment and air-to-air missiles their very high relative speeds and long-range detect and attack capabilities seemed to rule out any old style dog fights. For tactical operations, fighter-bombers capable of carrying nuclear bombs or large amounts of conventional weapons became the principal combat aircraft of most air forces. This trend was reversed by lessons from the Vietnam and Middle East wars. It was recognised that the defeat of enemy fighter force through air combat was still the imminent requirement. Designed from outset as an air superiority fighter, the F-15 Eagle was first flown in 1972, with production deliveries commencing in 1975. Initial single-seat F-15A fighters and two-seat F-15B trainers have been followed since 1979 by single-seat F-15C fighters and two-seat F-15Ds with improved radar, additional internal fuel capacity and provision for carrying two external conformal tanks. Instead of fuel, these can accommodate various types of avionics and other electronic equipment. Armament includes advanced fire control radar combined with air-to-air missiles for all weather interception. Although these F-15s can also fulfil ground attack tasks, McDonnell Douglas has developed an all-weather interdiction version of improved air-to-ground capability while retaining air superiority performance. Known as F-15E, these Enhanced Eagles are intended to replace F-111 fighter-bombers in USAF service.

Production orders of all F-15 Eagle versions total 1472 aircraft for the USAF. **Span** 13.05 m (42 ft 9¾ in) **Length** 19.43 m (63 ft 9 in) **Max speed** Mach 2.5 +

Left: F-15Cs of 19th TFW photographed from KC-135 tanker in October 1979. 105 mm f5.6 + ²/₃ 1/250 KM

Right: F-15C loops with 6 g pull-up, photographed from two-seat F-15D in July 1980. 50 mm f5.6 + ²/₃ 1/250 KM

General Dynamics F-16 Fighting Falcon Designed for the USAF Lightweight Fighter experimental programme, the F-16 was evolved as one of the most manoeuvrable fighters ever built. Although lacking all-weather combat capability of the F-15 Eagle, it costs about 50 per cent less and has also attracted many foreign customers.

F-16A from Hill AFB being refuelled by KC-135 in October 1980. 50 mm f5.6 1/250 KM

General Dynamics F-16 Fighting Falcon Advanced technologies in the F-16 include the use of composites in its construction, fly-by-wire flight control, reduced static stability and blended wing-fuselage aerodynamics with forebody strakes. Large underfuselage air intake is another unique F-16 design feature.

F-16A of 332 Sqn, Royal Netherlands Air Force, displays its 40th Anniversary tail markings at the Air Tatoo in July 1983.   400 mm f5.6 + 1/500 KR

General Dynamics F-16 Fighting Falcon First F-16 to enter operational service was delivered to the USAF's 388th TFW in January 1979 and many TAC, USAFE, PACAF and AFRES units are converting to the F-16 from F-4 Phantom and A-7 Corsair II. Total F-16 production is anticipated to exceed 3000 aircraft.

Span 9.45 m (31 ft 10 in) **Length** (overall) 15.09 m (49 ft 5⅞ in)
Max speed Mach 2.0

F-16A Fighting Falcon of 388th TFW during Exercise Maple Flag at Cold Lake AB, Canada, in June 1981.   28 mm f8 1/500 KR

General Dynamics F-16XL (F-16E) Advanced technology development of the F-16 series to new configuration featuring a 'cranked-arrow' wing which allows considerable performance improvement. Two development aircraft are now undergoing tests.

F-16XL roll-out ceremony at the General Dynamics plant in July 1982. 180 mm f5.6 1/500 KR

13

McDonnell Douglas F-18 Hornet Like the F-16 Fighting Falcons of the USAF, the F-18 Hornets are used by the US Navy to supplement more expensive operational types as A-4 Skyhawk and A-7 Corsair II replacements.

The first development F-18 Hornet on a test flight accompanied by an F-4 Phantom II from the Patuxent River Naval Air Test Centre, photographed from KC-130 in May 1982.   105 mm f5.6 + ⅓ 1/250 KM

McDonnell Douglas F-18 Hornet Although not as fast as some contemporaries, the F-18 Hornet possesses outstanding manoeuvrability and all weather combat/attack capability. RF-18 reconnaissance version equipped with cameras and sensors in now under evaluation. **Span** 11.43 m (37 ft 6 in)

Length 17.07 m (56 ft 0 in) **Max speed** Mach 1.8+
TF-18 two-seat trainer as demonstrated at the Paris Air Show in June 1981. 400 mm f5.6 + ⅓ 1/500 KR

Northrop F-20 Tigershark Developed as successor to the F-5E Tiger II export fighter, the F-20 was first flown in September 1982. Its F404 turbojet engine develops 70 per cent more power than F-5E's two J85 units and give the Tigershark significantly improved flight performance compared to the F-5E.

Span (over missiles) 8.53 m (27 ft 11⅞ in) **Length** (overall) 14.17 m (46 ft 6 in)
Max speed Mach 2.0

F-20 Tigershark at Edwards AFB in February 1983.
300 mm f5.6 + ⅓ 1/500 KR

Northrop F-5E Tiger II An advanced version of the F-5 Freedom Fighter, the Tiger II is an uncomplicated tactical air superiority fighter. Both single-seat F-5E and two-seat F-5F are in operational service in many countries, while the USAF and US Navy use the F-5E as 'aggressor' for air combat training.

Span 8.13 m (26 ft 8 in) **Length** 14.45 m (47 ft 4¾ in) **Max speed** Mach 1.6

F-5E simulating MiG 'aggressor' aircraft during Exercise Cape Thunder in the Philippines, photographed from T-33 in October 1980.
50 mm f5.6 + ⅓ 1/250 KM

17

Northrop F-5 Freedom Fighter A very successful small lightweight supersonic fighter. Substantially cheaper than its contemporaries of similar performance, large numbers of the F-5A to F-5D versions have been exported to 15 nations. **Span** 7.70 m (25 ft 3 in) **Length** 14.38 m (47 ft 2 in) **Max speed** Mach 1.4

Canadian Armed Forces' CF-5Bs displaying three different camouflage schemes in May 1981.   50 mm f5.6 + ⅓ 1/250 KM

McDonnell Douglas F-4 Phantom II Developed for the US Navy as carrier-borne fighter, the F-4 Phantom II was subsequently operated by the USAF and many foreign air forces. Its total production run exceeded that of any other Western supersonic fighter.

RAF's Phantom FRG.2 (F-4M) in grey low-visibility colour scheme at RAF Conigsby in June 1981.   180 mm f5.6 1/500 KR

McDonnell Douglas F-4 Phantom II Evolved to meet a US Navy requirement for an all-weather fleet defence fighter, the two-seat F-4 was chosen in preference to the single-seat single-engined Vought F8U-3. Noteworthy technical aspects incorporated in the F-4 construction included movable ramps in engine inlet ducts for different speed ranges, boundary layer control on both leading and trailing edge flaps, semi-recessed installation of Sparrow missiles and extensive use of titanium in primary structural members. At the time of its debut the F-4 had the longest-ranging radar in the world and gained fame as the first carrier-borne fighter to have higher performance than contemporary land-based fighters by establishing the absolute world records for maximum speed at high and low level, altitude and time-to-height. Sufficient engine power enables the F-4 to carry considerable ground-attack weapon payload, and this

versability led to the world-wide use of this aircraft. Total Phantom II production amounted to 5197 aircraft, of which 691 were of the FR-4 tactical reconnaissance version. Equipped with cameras, sideways-looking radar and IR line-scan system in its redesigned nose section, the FR-4 has all-weather and night reconnaissance capabilities. **Span** 11.70 m (38 ft 4¾ in) **Length** 19.16 m (62 ft 10½ in) **Max speed** Mach 2.4

Above left: *F-4C of Hawaii ANG photographed during formation loop in April 1982.   50 mm f5.6 + ½ 1/250 KM*

Above right: *Minnesota ANG RF-4C over Lake Michigan in May 1981.   50 mm f5.6 + ½ 1/250 KM*

Right: *US Marine Corps' F-4Ss in low-visibility camouflage, taken from an OM-10M over the Atlantic in August 1982. 50 mm f5.6 + ½ 1/250 KM*

McDonnell Douglas F-4 Phantom II Designed air combat armament of the Phantom II comprises two semi-active radar-homing medium-range Sparrow missiles or four IR-homing short-range Sidewinder or Falcon missiles, but later F-4Es for the USAF were also fitted with a nose-mounted 20 mm Vulcan cannon for close-combat fighting.

Camouflaged F-4EJ taking off during JASDF's annual weapon meet at Komatsu AB in November 1983.   400 mm f5.6 + ⅓ 1/500 KR

McDonnell Douglas F-4G 'Wild Weasel' Phantom II The F-4G is a modified F-4E fitted with electronic warfare equipment enabling it to detect, identify and locate enemy ground radars and to fire weapons for their suppression. Known as 'Wild Weasel' missions by the USAF, primary weapons used on these operations include anti-radiation missiles.

Reflecting the evening sun, an F-4G returns from a training mission at George AFB in November 1978.   300 mm f4.5 1/500 KR

General Dynamics F-111 F-111 is the world's first operational variable-geometry warplane and one of the most powerful fighter-bombers extant. Although its production terminated in 1967, F-111s still form the nucleus of the USAF tactical striking force. **Span** 19.20/9.74 m (63 ft 0 in/31 ft 11⅜ in)

Length 22.40 m (73 ft 6 in) **Max speed** Mach 2.5
F-111s off Ireland on route from the United Kingdom to USA, photographed from KC-135 tanker in September 1980. 105 mm f5.6 1/250 KM

Grumman (General Dynamics) EF-111A Raven A total of 42 F-111s are being converted by Grumman for electronic warfare missions as EF-111A. Fitted with AN/ALQ-99E jamming system and other avionics, EF-111A tasks are the surveillance and jamming of enemy radars and communications support of US tactical strike force.

EF-111A in aerial refuelling training over Colorado, photographed from Utah ANG's KC-135 in August 1982. 105 mm f5.6 1/250 KM

General Dynamics FB-111A FB-111A was developed from the F-111 fighter to replace the B-58 Hustler and earlier versions of the B-52 Stratofortress bombers. Like the F-111, the FB-111A is capable of supersonic speed at about 60 m (200 ft) above the ground level on automatic control. Its weapon loads comprise six nuclear-tipped missiles or four nuclear bombs.

F-111A taking off from Cold Lake AB, Canada, during Exercise Maple Flag in May 1981.   400 mm f5.6 + ²/₃ 1/500 KR

Geeral Dynamics F-106 Delta Dart Developed by Convair in the mid-1950s for the defence of US mainland, the F-106 Delta Dart was equipped with the world's most advanced fire control system for its day. Although dated, some F-106s still serve with certain USAF and ANG units. **Span** 11.67 m (38 ft 3½ in) **Length** 21.56 m (70 ft 8¾ in) **Max speed** Mach 2.3

Line-up of F-106As in a rainy night at Tyndall AFB during the William Tell Meet in September 1978.   28 mm f5.6 Auto KR

27

Fairchild F-105 Thunderchief Evolved by Republic in the mid-1950s, the
F-105 Thunderchief was one of the best fighter-bombers at that time. It played a
major role in the air war over Vietnam, but the last operational single-seat
F-105Ds and two-seat F-105Fs are now about to leave the active service.

Span 10.65 m (34 ft 11¼ in) **Length** 20.43 m (67 ft 0¼ in) **Max speed** Mach 2.03
*Bombs away! F-105D in action over the Utah Test and Training Range in
October 1980.   50 mm f4 + ½ 1/500 KM*

Lockheed F-104 Starfighter F-104 is the world's first Mach 2 fighter and unquestionably one of the most outstanding combat aircraft of its era. Although the procurement for the USAF was limited, this high-performance fighter served with many foreign air forces. **Span** 6.68 m (21 ft 11 in) **Length** 16.69 m (54 ft 9 in)

Max speed Mach 2.2

Generating vapour trails, Canadian Armed Forces' CF-104s climb after a hard 4.5 pull-out in August 1980.   50 mm f5.6 + ⅓ 1/250 KM

29

Vought F-8 Crusader The world's first supersonic carrier-borne fighter, F-8 Crusader has now been retired from the US Navy service except for the RF-8G reconnaissance version with Reserve units. The F-8 is still in first-line service with the French Navy and Philippines Air Force. **Span** 10.87 m (35 ft 8 in) **Length**

16.61 m (54 ft 6 in) **Max speed** Mach 1.7
RF-8G in the Photo Finish Meet at Gulfport airport, USA, in October 1981.
300 mm f5.6 + ²/₃ 1/500 KR

McDonnell Douglas A-4 Skyhawk Small but mighty, the A-4 Skylark is one of the most successful carrier and land-based attack aircraft, with its production totalling 2960 over a period of 25 years. Although now retired from US carrier operations, A-4s are still being used by the USMC and many foreign air forces.

Span 8.38 m (27 ft 6 in) **Length** 12.27 m (40 ft 3¼ in) **Max speed** Mach 0.94
US Marine Corps' A-4Ms at Kadena air base, Japan, in July 1980.
400 mm f8 1/500 KR

31

Grumman A-6 Intruder First flown in 1960, the A-6 Intruder is a carrier-borne long-range all-weather low-level strike aircraft. The advanced A-6E version is still in production, and the improved A-6F with new avionics and more powerful engines is to be developed. **Span** 16.15 m (53 ft 0 in) **Length** 16.64 m (54 ft 7 in)

Max speed Mach 0.86
*US Marine Corps' A-6Es over the Atlantic in August 1981.
50 m f5.6 + ½ 1/250 KM*

Grumman EA-6B Prowler An electronic warfare version of the A-6 Intruder, developed in the late 1960s. Its 1.37 m (4 ft 6 in) longer fuselage nose section accommodates two additional crew members, and an extensive array of electronic detection and jamming devices is carried internally and in pods.

An EA-6B coming in to land aboard USS Ranger *in April 1980. Note the three radar jamming pods under the fuselage and wings.*   *400 mm f8 1/500 KR*

33

Vought A-7 Corsair II Selected by the US Navy as successor to A-4 Skyhawk, the A-7 Corsair II entered service in 1967. It was adopted by the USAF to augment its tactical air power, and some were exported to Greece and Portugal.

A-7Ds of the New Mexico ANG, photographed from KC-135 in August 1982. 105 mm f5.5 + ⅓ 1/250 KM

Vought A-7 Corsair II Its basic design was derived from the F-8 fighter and modified for subsonic operations with emphasis on range and load-carrying. Six underwing pylons can take a wide variety of weapons while two fuselage pylons are for air-to-air missiles. **Span** 11.80 m (38 ft 9 in) **Length** 14.06 m (46 ft 1½ in)

Max speed Mach 0.94

A-7Es await take-off orders on the deck of USS Ranger *during Exercise Rimpack in April 1980.   400 m f8 1/500 KR*

Fairchild A-10 Thunderbolt II Designed specifically for close air support missions, the A-10 can carry up to 7258 kg (16,000 lb) of weapons and is fitted with a 30 mm seven-barrel cannon to combat a wide variety of ground targets, including tanks.

A-10A at the Abbotsford Air Show, Canada, in August 1979.
300 m f8 1/500 KR

Fairchild A-10 Thunderbolt II The A-10 was evolved to meet the threat posed by massive Soviet armoured forces based in Eastern Europe. In case of war, A-10s would deploy on small forward-location bases to fly repeated attacks. **Span** 17.53 m (57 ft 6 in) **Length** 16.26 m (53 ft 4 in)

Max speed 717 km/h (439 mph)

Realistic exercises: while one A-10 comes in to land, its wingman watches the surrounding area. Thunderbolt IIs of the Massachusettes ANG, photographed in September 1979.   50 mm f8 1/500 KR

37

Panavia Tornado An international development, the Tornado multi-role combat aircraft is now in service with the air forces in Britain, West Germany and Italy. To fulfil six major requirements – close air support/battlefield interdiction, interdiction/counter-air strike, air superiority, interception, naval strike and reconnaissance – its relatively compact two-seat, twin-engined design with variable-geometry wings was formulated. As it is impossible to achieve the highest performance in every aspect, Tornado's design is emphasised on all-weather low-level high-speed strike with extremely high accuracy, and on STOL capability which provides it with operational flexibility and improved survivability on the ground. In addition to the basic IDS (Interdiction/Strike) for all three nations, an ADV (Air Defence Variant) has been developed specifically for Britain. Known in the RAF service as Tornado F.2, the ADV is 80 per cent identical to the IDS (Tornado GR.1 in the RAF service), its main differences being longer fuselage, new long-range air intercept radar and semi-recessed mounts for Sky Flash medium-range missiles in addition to pylon-mounted Sidewinder short-range missiles.

The first Tornado prototype made its maiden flight in 1974, and delivery of the IDS to operational units commenced in 1982. Tornado F.2 ADV is scheduled to be in service by 1985. Planned production amounts to 809 aircraft (including four pre-production aircraft to be refurbished), but additional procurement by the three nations and export orders are being sought.
Span 13.90/8.60 m (45 ft 7¼ in/28 ft 2½ in) **Length** 16.70 m (54 ft 9½ in) **Max speed** Mach 2.1

Facing page: *Tornado F.2 prototype armed with four Sky Flash missiles executing a steep turn after take-off at the Farnborough Air Show in September 1980.* 400 m f5.6 + ⅔ 1/500 KR

Above, left: *Tornado GR.1 demonstrating its bomb-carrying capabilities at the Farnborough Air show in September 1980.* 600 mm f5.6 + ⅔ 1/500 KR

Left: *High-speed fly-past by Tornado GR.1 of No. 9 Squadron, RAF, at the Farnborough Air Show in September 1982.* 400 m f5.6 + ⅔ 1/500 KR

Panavia Tornado To accomplish deep-penetration strike missions, the Tornado IDS has outstanding payload/range performance and is designed for high-speed terrain-following flight, while its sophisticated avionics system provides precise navigation and first-strike hit capability.

West German Navy's Tornado IDS armed with four Kormoran anti-shipping missiles at the Paris Air Show in July 1980.   400 m f5.6 + ²/₃ 1/500 KR

SEPECAT Jaguar Supersonic strike fighter jointly developed by Britain and France, the Jaguar has been in service since 1973. It outstanding features are high-speed preformance and accurate bomb/navigation capabilities.
Span 8.69 m (28 ft 6 in) **Length** 16.83 m (55 ft 2½ in) **Max speed** Mach 1.6

Jaguar of No. 2 Squadron, RAF, retracts its landing gear immediately after becoming airborne at the Farnborough Air Show in September 1980. 400 m f5.6 + ²/₃ 1/500 KR

41

Dassault-Bréguet/Dornier Alpha Jet This small two-seat twin-jet was designed jointly by French/German teams to meet the requirement for an advanced trainer for the French Air Force and a light tactical strike aircraft for the Luftwaffe. For combat missions, the Alpha Jet can carry a 30 mm cannon pod and two tons of attack weapons. **Span** 9.11 m (29 ft 10¾ in) **Length** 13.23 m (43 ft 5 in) **Max speed** Mach 0.85
Luftwaffe Alpha Jet at the Air Tattoo in June 1981. 400 mm f6 + ²/₃ 1/500 KR

British Aerospace Hawk It is now popular to use trainers for light attack missions by smaller air forces. The BAe Hawk is one of the most powerful aircraft in its class and it is planned to develop a single-seat pure strike version. **Span** 9.40 m (30 ft 9¾ in) **Length** 11.96 m (36 ft 7¾ in) **Max speed** Mach 0.85

BAe Hawk from No 1 Tactical Weapons Unit, RAF Brawdy, demonstrates a slow roll at the Air Tattoo in July 1981.   400 mm f5.6 1/500 KR

BAe Lightning Of unique design, featuring 'notched delta' wing planform and twin 'over and under' engine layout, the Lightning was once the world's fastest climbing interceptor. Now nearing the end of its service life, the Lightning will be replaced by Tornado ADVs in RAF service from mid-1980s.

Span 10.62 m (34 ft 10 in) **Length** 16.84 m (55 ft 3 in) **Max speed** Mach 2.27

Lightning F.3 in grey camouflage scheme at the Air Tattoo in July 1983.
400 mm f5.6 + ²/₃ 1/500 KR

BAe Buccaneer The Buccaneer was developed in the late 1950s to meet a Royal Navy requirement for a carrier-borne strike aircraft with emphasis on low-level transonic performance. After the retirement of RN carriers Buccaneers have been operated by the RAF in strike and anti-shipping roles.

Span 13.41 m (44 ft 0 in) **Length** 19.33 m (63 ft 5 in) **Max speed** Mach 0.92
Buccaneer S.2 in high-speed low-level pass during the Air Tattoo in June 1979. 400 mm f5.6 + ⅓ 1/500 KR

45

BAe Harrier Harrier is the world's first operational V/STOL strike fighter, powered by a single Pegasus vectored-thrust turbofan engine. After protracted development it entered RAF service in 1969 and was also adopted by the US Marine Corps as AV-8A. **Span** 7.70 m (25 ft 3¼ in) **Length** 13.87 m (45 ft 6 in)

Max speed Mach 0.95

AV-8As peel off, displaying their underwing ordnance, taken from an OM-4M in August 1982.   28mm f5.6 + ²/₃ 1/250 KM

McDonnell Douglas/BAe AV-8B Harrier To improve the Harrier's payload/range capabilities, the AV-8B version was developed for the USMC as a joint American-British effort. It features completely redesigned wing planform and uses advanced composite materials for its overall structure. The RAF will also operate AV-8B as Harrier GR.5.

AV-8B during tests at NAS Patuxent River in August 1982.
300 mm f8 1/500 KR

47

BAe Sea Harrier One of the most revolutionary features of V/STOL aircraft is their capability to operate from small ships. The Sea Harrier built for the Royal Navy has similar general flight performance to the RAF version but incorporates new search radar which provides great improvement in air-to-air and anti-

ship effectiveness.

Sea Harrier FRS.1s that won fame in the Falklands conflict in hover at the Farnborough Air Show in September 1982. 300 mm f5.6 + ½ 1/500 KR

Dassault-Bréguet Super Etendard French multi-purpose carrier-based fighter. Aircraft exported to Argentina gained reputation flying anti-shipping strikes with Exocet ASM missiles during the Falklands conflict.
Span 9.60 m (31 ft 6 in) **Length** 14.31 m (46 ft 11½ in) **Max speed** Mach 1.05

French Navy's Super Etendards demonstrate the buddy system air refuelling at the Air Tattoo in June 1981.   400 mm f5.6 + ⅓ 1/500 KR

Dassault-Bréguet Super Mirage 4000 Twin-engined fighter, basically a scaled-up development of the Mirage 2000, evolved without French Air Force requirement. Privately funded prototype was flown in 1979 in anticipation of export orders, but the possibility of production is now minimal.

Super Mirage 4000 at the Farnborough Air Show in September 1982.
400 mm f8 1/500 KR

Dassault-Bréguet Mirage 2000 While delta wing configuration was gradually thought of as dated due to certain inherent disadvantages, the Mirage 2000 revived this formula to achieve high manoeuvrability by using latest technology. There is also a two-seat strike version armed with nuclear-tipped missiles.

Span 9.00 m (29 ft 6 in) **Length** 15.33 m (50 ft 3½ in) **Max speed** Mach 2.3
Mirage 2000 carrying four air-to-air missiles at the Paris Air Show in July 1981. 300 mm f5.6 + ²/₃ 1/500 KR

Dassault-Bréguet Mirage F.1 Primarily an all-weather interceptor, the Mirage F.1 also has considerable ground attack capability, and a tactical reconnaissance version is also in service. **Span** 8.40 m (27 ft 6¾ in) **Length** 15.00 (49 ft 2½ in) **Max speed** Mach 2.3

Mirage F.1C for the Royal Jordanian Air Force at the Paris Air Show in July 1983.   400 mm f5.6 + ²/₃ 1/500 KR

Dassault-Bréguet Mirage III Mirage III was one of the best-selling fighters during 1960s and '70s. Many versions are in service worldwide and to extend its production run, which has already passed the 1400 mark, a significantly improved Mirage IIING version was developed in 1982.

Span 8.22 m (26 ft 11½ in) **Length** 15.03 m (49 ft 3½ in) **Max speed** Mach 2.2
Mirage IIIE fighter-bomber at the Air Tattoo in July 1979.
400 mm f5.6 + ⅔ 1/500 KR

Mitsubishi F-1 Evolved from the T-2 supersonic advanced trainer, the F-1 is notable as the first Japanese tactical fighter since the Second World War. Its primary role is anti-shipping strike, but it can also perform close support and intercept tasks. **Span** 7.88 m (25 ft 10¼ in) **Length** 17.84 m (58 ft 6¼ in)

Max speed Mach 1.6
F-1 with 'shark-mouthed' bomblet dispenser during the JASDF fighter weapon competition at Komatsu AB in November 1983.   300 mm f5.6 + ²/₃ 1/500 KR

SAAB 37 Viggen The Swedish Viggen multi-mission combat aircraft achieves Mach 2.0 and outstanding STOL capabilities by means of its novel delta wing/canard configuration. Use of reverse thrust is also unique in fighter community. **Span** 10.60 m (34 ft 9¼ in) **Length** 15.58 m (51 ft 4½ in)

Max speed Mach 2.1
With its reverse thrust blowing water off the runway, an SAAB 37 Viggen demonstrates its short landing capabilities at the Farnborough Air Show in September 1980.   300 mm f5.6 + ²/₃ 1/500 KR

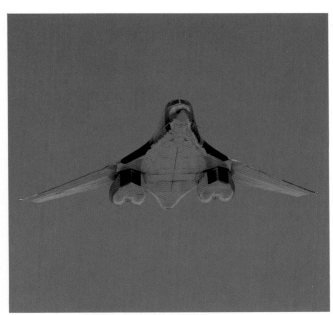

Rockwell International B-1 During the Cold War period both West and East made frantic efforts to develop long-range strategic bombers which were regarded as the decisive deterrent power after the introduction of the nuclear bomb. The USAF's B-52 bomber, still in service, is one of the products of these efforts. The subsequent growth of the ICBM and SLBM weapons weakened the relative status of strategic bombers as the deterrent force and reduced the need for expensive new bombers. As a result, the ambitious Mach 3.0 B-70 programme remained only in experimental stage and studies of the new generation bombers were prolonged.

At last, after two decades of dependence on the subsonic B-52, development of its successor commenced in 1969. Designated B-1, the new bomber was first flown in 1974, but all further work on it was cancelled in 1977 by the Carter administration. This decision was reversed by President Reagan who approved plans to produce 100 B-1Bs, improved version of the already completed B-1A.

The most important operational feature of the B-1 is its very low-level high-subsonic flight capability through the use of the variable-geometry wings and advanced avionics. To penetrate the enemy defence network, the B-1 will also employ highly sophisticated electronic jamming systems. Though smaller than the B-52, the B-1 can carry 24 nuclear-tipped attack missiles or 12 high-yield nuclear bombs in its weapons bay. At a later date, provisions will also be made for the external carriage of 14 long-range ALCMs with 16 similar missiles internally. The first B-1Bs are scheduled for delivery to the SAC in June 1985, the current order for 100 aircraft being completed in 1988.

Span 41.67/23.83 m (136 ft 8½ in/78 ft 2½ in) **Length** 44.83 m (147 ft 0 in) **Max speed** Mach 1.2

Left: *B-1A approaches its tanker for refuelling on the way back from the United Kingdom, photographed from KC-135A of the Maine ANG in September 1982. 105mm f5.6 + ⅔ 1/250 KM*

Upper left: *B-1A in high speed configuration over Edwards AFB in August 1982. 400 mm f8 1/500 KR*

Lower left: *Pre-flight check of B-1A at Edwards AFB in August 1982. 300 mm f8 1/500 KR*

Boeing B-52 Stratofortress First B-52 strategic bombers became operational with the USAF in 1955, and their production ended in 1962. Since that time the basic design has been progressively updated and the Stratofortress still forms the nucleus of the SAC bomber force. **Span** 56.42 m (185 ft 1½ in)

Length 48.03 m (157 ft 7 in) **Max speed** 0.95
With Canadian cumulonimbus clouds in the background, B-52G climbs into the sky at the Abbotsford Air Show in August 1980.   180mm f8 1/500 KR

Lockheed TR-1 Derived from the U-2 'spy plane', the TR-1 is intended for stand-off battlefield surveillance with special electronic sensors in an interchangable nose section and fuselage and wing pods. It is also capable of high-altitude reconnaissance missions like its predecessor.

Span 31.39 m (103 ft 0 in) **Length** 19.20 m (63 ft 0 in)
Max speed 692 + km/h (430 + mph)
TR-1A at the Farnborough Air Show in September 1982.
400 mm f5.6 + ²/₃ 1/500 KR

Lockheed SR-71 Blackbird SR-71 is the world's fastest and highest-flying strategic reconnaissance aircraft. To endure Mach 3 aerodynamic heat, which can be as high as 565.5°C (1050°F) in some places, most of its structure is made of titanium, while corrugations over the wings surfaces control thermal distortion.

SR-71A approaches to refuel over the snow-capped Rocky mountains, taken from KC-135Q tanker in March 1981.   105mm f5.6 + ⅓ 1/250 KM

Lockheed SR-71 The Lockheed A-11 prototype first flew in 1962 and delivery of the SR-71 production aircraft to 9th SRW began in 1966. Its mission is photographic and electronic reconnaissance of Communist countries and detachments of 9th SRW are deployed in the UK and Japan.

Span 16.95 m (55 ft 7 in) **Length** 32.74 m (107 ft 5 in) **Max speed** 3.3
An impressive view of an SR-71A at Beale AFB, USA, in March 1981. 300 mm f5.6 1/500 KR

Boeing E-3 Sentry The Sentry is an AWACS (Airborne Warning and Control System) based on the Boeing 707 commercial transport airframe. Powerful rotating radar enclosed in a large disc-shaped fairing above the rear fuselage enables long-range surveillance over land or water. E-3s will also be used by NATO forces. **Span** 44.42 m (145 ft 9 in) **Length** 46.61 m (152 ft 11 in) **Max speed** Mach 0.83

USAF's E-3A during Exercise Maple Flag in June 1981.
300 mm f5.6 + ⅔ 1/500 KR

Grumman E-2 Hawkeye The E-2 early warning aircraft was developed for US carrier operations. Each US Navy aircraft carrier has four Hawkeyes, while Israel, Japan and Egypt use E-2s for land-based operations.
Span 24.58 m (80 ft 7 in) **Length** 17.55 m (57 ft 7 in)

Max speed 582 km/h (362 mph)
Folding its wings, JASDF's E-2C taxis in on the snow-covered Misawa AB runway in February 1984. 400 mm f5.6 + ⅔ 1/500 KR

Lockheed P-3 Orion The Orion is the US Navy's land-based maritime patrol aircraft. Evolved from the Electra turboprop commercial transport, the P-3 design has been continutally updated and the capabilities of its anti-submarine sensors and data processing greatly improved. **Span** 30.38 m (99 ft 8 in)

Length 35.61 m (116 ft 10 in) **Max speed** 761 km/h (473 mph)
P-3C approaches one of the parallel runways at Kadena AB, while an A-4M is simultaneously coming in on the other one, July 1980.   300 mm f8 1/500 KR

Lockheed S-3 Viking Though relatively small, this carrier-borne anti-submarine aircraft carries a whole array of submarine detection sensors and attack weapons. S-3 production was completed in 1978, but avionics modernisation programme is proceeding to extend its service effectiveness.

Span 20.93 m (68 ft 8 in) **Length** 16.26 m (53 ft 4 in)
Max speed 834 km/h (518 mph)

An S-3A Viking returns to USS Langley *during Exercise Rimpack in April 1980.   300 mm f8 1/500 KR*

Kawasaki P-2J The P-2J anti-submarine aircraft is a development of the Lockheed P-2H Neptune. Change of power plant to T64 turboprops and fitting of modern search and control systems resulted in a major improvement of operational capabilities, and a total of 83 P-2Js were built.

Span 29.78 m (97 ft 8½ in) **Length** 29.23 m (95 ft 10¾ in)
Max speed 557 km/h (346 mph)
JMSDF's P-2J taking off from Atsugi AB in December 1980.
400 mm f.6 + ²/₃ 1/500 KR

Shin Meiwa PS-1 In addition to search radar, MAD and sonobuoy systems the PS-1 anti-submarine flying boat is also equipped with a large dunking sonar. To use its sonar at rough seas the PS-1 is designed to have enhanced STOL capability. **Span** 33.15 m (108 ft 8¾ in) **Length** 33.46 m (109 ft 9¼ in)

Max speed 526 km/h (327 mph)
Three PS-1s in echelon formation, photographed from another PS-1 in January 1983. 105 mm f5.6 1/500 KM

67

Dassault-Bréguet Atlantic The Atlantic maritime patrol aircraft was developed as P-2 Neptune replacement for the navies of NATO nations. Production of 87 Atlantics was completed in 1973, but an improved version with modern sensors and avionics is to be produced for the French Navy. **Span** 36.30 (119 ft 1 in)

Length 37.75 m (104 ft 2 in) **Max speed** 657 km/h (409 mph)
West German Navy's Atlantic in low-level flight at the Air Tattoo in June 1979. 300 mm f5.6 + ²/₃ 1/500 KR

BAe Nimrod The original Nimrod was derived from Comet 4, the final version of the world's first jet airliner. Principal changes included added underfuselage pannier to accommodate the weapons bay and operational equipment, and a fin-tip pod with ECM gear. **Span** 35.00 m (114 ft 10 in)

Length 38.63 m (126 ft 9 in) **Max speed** 926 km/h (575 mph)
Nimrod MR.2 with aerial refuelling probe at the Air Tattoo in July 1983.
300 mm f5.6 + 2/3 1/500 KR

69

BAe Nimrod Of the 46 Nimrods built, 11 are being converted to an early warning (AEW) version. Unlike the American AEW aircraft which use the rotodome, the Nimrod AEW.3 carries radar in nose and tail positions to achieve 360 degrees surveillance capability.

Nimrod AEW.3 approaches to land at the Farnborough Air Show in September 1980, giving close-up view of its impressive nose radome.
300 mm f5.6 + ²/₃ 1/500 KR

BAe VC 10 Total of four VC 10 and five Super VC 10 airliners are being converted by British Aerospace to VC 10 K.Mk2 and K.Mk.3 three-point aerial refuellers to augment the RAF tanker force. The first VC 10 K.Mk.2 entered service in 1984. **Span** 44.55 m (146 ft 2 in) **Length** 48.36 m (158 ft 8 in)

Max speed 909 km/h (568 mph)
The first converted VC 10 K.Mk.2, serial ZA141, in flight in September 1982, with its central refuelling probe extended. 300 m f4.5 1/500 KR

71

McDonnell Douglas KC-10 Extender The Extender is a military tanker/cargo transport version of the DC-10 wide-bodied commercial airliner, equipped with refuelling boom and a nose reel system. Deliveries to the USAF began in 1981 and 60 aircraft are on order. **Span** 50.41 m (165 ft 4½ in)

Length 55.35 m (181 ft 7 in) **Max speed** 925 km/h (575 mph)

KC-10 leaves position after refuelling from a KC-135 during trans-Atlantic flight in September 1982.   50mm f5.6 + ²/₃ 1/250 KM

Boeing KC-135 Stratotanker KC-135 is the world's first jet-powered tanker and a total of 732 aircraft were built during the period 1956 to 1965. To extend its service life the USAF plans to re-engine a number of KC-135s. Derivatives of the KC-135 are used for strategic and weather reconnaissance and as airborne command posts. **Span** 39.88 m (130 ft 10 in) **Length** 41.53 m (136 ft 3 in) **Max speed** 945 km/h (587 mph)

KC-135A photographed from the receiver in September 1982.
105 mm f5.6 + ²/₃ 1/250 KM

73

Lockheed C-5 Galaxy The Galaxy is the world's largest military freighter, capable of airlifting 100 tons of payload. With its unique front and rear loading facilities the C-5 can easily handle even large bulky equipment. Total of 81 C-5As were built in 1968-1973 and production of 50 C-5Bs is planned.

Span 67.88 m (222 ft 8½ in) **Length** 75.54 m (247 ft 10 in)
Max speed 919 km/h (571 mph)
Line-up of C-5As on Clark AB the Philippines in October 1980.
300 mm f5.6 + ²/₃ 1/250 KR

Lockheed C-141 Starlifter Together with C-5 Galaxy, the Starlifter forms the strategic airlift force of the USAF. Total of 284 C-141As were built by 1968 and most were later converted to C-141B with 'stretched' fuselages and added in-flight refuelling capability. **Span** 48.74 m (159 ft 11 in)

Length 51.29 m (168 ft 3½ in) **Max speed** 919 km/h (571 mph)

C-141B in the dark European One camouflage scheme taking off from Hickam AB, Hawaii, in April 1982.   400 mm f5.6 + ²/₃ 1/500 KR

Lockheed C-130 Hercules First flown in 1954, the C-130 Hercules is the USAF's first tactical transport powered by turboprop engines. It has become known as the aircraft that established the standard design formula for tactical transports. No other military transport aircraft is in such widespread use throughout the world. Production of the C-130 already exceeds the 1700 mark, and it is quite feasible that C-130s will still be built in the 1990s. In addition to its original airlift mission, the versatile design of the Hercules allows it to fulfil various other tasks, such as refuelling, aerial survey, search and rescue, maritime patrol, drone launch, command communications, battlefield command control, electronic warfare, mine laying, weather reconnaissance, fire fighting and air-snatch satellite recovery. Other versions produced include the Hercules gunship, ski

undercarriage and 'stretched' fuselage variants, and commercial models. **Span** 40.41 m (132 ft 7 in) **Length** 29.78 m (97 ft 9 in) **Max speed** 621 km/h (386 mph)

Left: *USAF CH-130P search and rescue aircraft refuels an HH-53C, taken from another HH-53C off the coast of Okinawa in January 1981.   105mm f5.6 + ½ 1/250 Km*

Upper left: *RAF's Hercules C.3, a 'stretched' model, demonstrates its agility by flying a steep turn after take-off at the Air Tattoo in July 1983   300 mm f5.6 + ⅓ 1/500 KR*

Upper right: *C-130E of the Californian ANG, photographed from the open rear cargo door of the leading aircraft in November 1981.   300 mm f5.6 + ⅔ 1/500 KR*

Transall C-160 This twin-turboprop transport was developed jointly by France and West Germany. Its production was completed with 178 aircraft in 1972, but restarted for the French Air Force in 1981. **Span** 40.00 m (131 ft 3 in) **Length** 32.40 m (106 ft 3½ in) **Max speed** 513 km/h (319 mph)

French Air Force C-160F transport at the Farnborough Air Show in September 1982. 300 mm f5.6 + ⅔ 1/500 KR

Kawasaki C-1 Developed as a replacement for the JASDF's aged Curtiss C-46s, the C-1 features unique quadruple-slotted flaps to provide STOL capability. It is also the world's first operational jet-powered tactical transport.
Span 30.60 m (100 ft 4¾ in) **Length** 29.00 m (95 ft 1¾ in)

Max speed 806 km/h (501 mph)
C-1 of the JASDF participating in paratroop exercises in January 1982.
180 mm f5.6 + ⅔ 1/500 KR

79